The Mormon Faith: A Theological Assessment

William W. Wells

Best regards
Bill

BooksByBill.biz

Copyright © 2010 by William W. Wells.

All rights reserved.

BooksByBill.biz
P.O. Box 20224
Fountain Valley, CA 92728-0224

Table of Contents

1. Introduction — 1
2. A Brief History of the Mormon Faith — 8
3. Sources of Mormon Theology — 18
4. Defining the Word *Christian* — 25
5. God and His Universe — 34
6. Humanity: Origins and Fall — 46
7. The Person of Jesus Christ — 53
8. The Nature of Our Salvation — 59
9. Theological Reflections — 63

Suggested Reading — 70

About the Author — 75

1. Introduction

In the 19th century, Christians and Mormons often fought. And, while most of those battles were verbal, some of them involved real guns and bullets that left some of the combatants dead. Thankfully, such physical fights have been relegated to the past. However, the verbal battles continue. For example, a book easily available on the Internet claims that, "… what the Mormons are propagating is a false god, false Jesus, and false gospel" and indicates that "… this incisive book clearly explains the Mormons' basic beliefs and sharply refutes their subtle heresies."[1]

Recently, a friend made the comment that you can't minister to those you don't love. I agree. And the tone of quotations from the previous paragraph doesn't sound like love to me.

During the last few years, a more peaceable group of orthodox Christians[2] and Mormons have begun meeting together to learn how to dialog in a "civil" manner. Participants have attempted to listen carefully and to speak gently and with respect. They have attempted to speak the truth as they see it, but without the stridency that has sometimes characterized past discussions. Moreover, Mormons and Christians have jointly published several books in the last few years.[3] The desire of the authors has been to help the public understand the similarities and differences between the two theological systems.

I would like to begin this short document by stating clearly that I respect those attempts. The Apostle Paul tells us to "speak the truth in love." Love would lead us to listen (or read) carefully and to speak (or write) without rancor or stridency. This short document is my attempt to participate in the written part of that dialog.

So what do I propose to add to this discussion? Briefly, I'd like to focus on the second part of Paul's admonition – that is, to speak the truth. The discussion hasn't, in some cases, been truly *joined*. At least, that's how it appears to me. The participants in such discussions – <u>both in person and in writing</u> – have focused so intently <u>on speaking and writing in love that they have avoided focusing on the differences between the two theological systems.</u>

I recently attended a dialog at a large church in Southern California. First, two gentlemen, an Evangelical and a Mormon, each spoke for 15 minutes about the nature of Jesus Christ. Then a second pair of participants, a Mormon and an Evangelical, each spoke for 15 minutes about the nature of salvation. Then, the four participants addressed questions to each other and offered replies for another 30 or 40 minutes.

The dialog was indeed civil – gentle and respectful as they planned. They acknowledged similarities between their positions – and yes, differences too. But in their concern to model civility and respect, they didn't really devote themselves to clarifying the differences between the two positions.

I'm guessing that most of those who attended the dialog came in order to increase their understanding of the differences between the two theological systems. They didn't come to listen to a panel of theologians deliver observations that could offend no one – which in my opinion is what they heard. Rather, they came to understand why Christians in general refuse to acknowledge that the Mormon Faith is actually Christian.[4]

ract # The Mormon Faith

What they heard instead was four men acknowledging that there are in fact some verbal similarities between the two systems – which there are. But because the dialog was never really *joined*, the audience had no opportunity for focusing on those distinctions. And I, for one, came away wishing the format had engendered more clarity than it did.

As I noted above, you can't minister to people you don't love. It just doesn't work. On the other hand, you can't minister to people you don't understand either. There is a place for careful thinking. There is a place for theological reflection.

This document is my response to sitting in the audience of that dialog. I will, as I've already indicated, attempt to model civility and respect in my writing. However, I would like to focus on the distinctions between the two theologies. And, while I will attempt to be civil, I will also be direct and to the point. I'd like to provide a very brief primer that will allow both Christians and Mormons to understand each other better. Personally, I'm an Evangelical. But I'm writing as an orthodox Christian, not particularly as an Evangelical. The distinctions I'd like to discuss are at the heart of the Christian Faith.

Note my assumption. I believe that ideas can be mutually exclusive. For example, if I say that today is Monday, I'm also saying that it is not Tuesday – and tacitly, I'm saying that anyone who asserts that it is Tuesday is simply wrong. But in today's culture, not everyone agrees that ideas can be mutually exclusive. And many would argue vehemently that religious ideas cannot – indeed, should not – be treated in that manner. I disagree – at least partially. To understand my perspective, think briefly about the claims of Muhammad and Joseph Smith.

In the 7th century, Muhammad claimed to have received an angelic visitor who brought him a message from God himself – in Arabic, the language of heaven. Muhammad claimed to have memorized the message. Later, he proclaimed the message to others as he was commanded to do. Muslims today believe that the *Qur'an* contains those revelations.

In the early 19th century, Joseph Smith, the founder of the Mormon faith, also claimed to have received an angelic visitor who directed him to a set of golden tablets that had been buried for about 1,500 years. He claimed to have dug them up, translated them and published them. Mormons view that publication, *The Book of Mormon*, as God's revelation.

The problem is: The teachings of the *Qur'an* and *The Book of Mormon* are utterly irreconcilable; they are mutually exclusive. Pretending that all religions say more or less the same thing is simply foolish. They don't.

Although I don't personally believe either claim, it is logically possible that one or the other is true. But it's not logically possible that they both are. And that means that at least one of them is a fabrication.

Informed orthodox Christians have consistently denied that Mormon theology is Christian at all. And I'm aware that Mormons find orthodox opposition to their faith perplexing, and yes, offensive. The purpose of this booklet is to explain why orthodox Christian theological leaders refuse to grant that Mormon theology is in fact Christian. I'm writing to both orthodox Christians and Mormons. In my opinion, both sides of this discussion, Christians and Mormons, need to understand conceptually the fundamental theological conflict between the two positions.

The pages that follow are, therefore, very focused. I intend to limit the scope of this booklet in several ways.

First, The question *Are Mormons Christians?* hides an ambiguity.[5] It could be asking, "Are Mormon believers actually Christians? Do they actually know God?" Or, it could be asking, "Is the Mormon church a member of the Christian community?" Or, it could be asking, "Is Mormon theology a legitimate theological expression of the Christian Faith?" Personally, I believe that it's inappropriate to ask the first question. An individual's relationship with God is the business of that individual and not mine. The second question is a minefield of ambiguity. One would need to begin by defining the phrase, "Christianity community." I wouldn't consider wading into that morass! Hence, I'll focus on the third question exclusively.

Tacitly, focusing on theology excludes a variety of related topics. *The Book of Mormon* contains historical material that is highly controversial. I'll ignore that controversy entirely. Smith's various accounts of his visions are hard to reconcile. I intend to ignore that problem. The Mormon Faith teaches a variety of theological ideas which are unique to them: Baptism for the dead, a tripartite view of heaven, and the possibility of eternal marriages. All of those ideas are beyond my purview. I intend to focus on the fundamental theological differences between the two systems of thought. If the orthodox Christian Faith and the Mormon Faith rest on mutually exclusive theological foundations, as I believe they do, then the issues I have just noted in this paragraph are simply irrelevant.

Finally, I do not intend to defend orthodoxy nor attack the Mormon Faith. Rather, I will focus simply on contrasting the two theological perspectives so that readers will be able to understand the conflict of ideas.

With that said, what follows?

- The second chapter provides a brief historical sketch of the Mormon Faith. Mormon readers will find this familiar territory and will be able to skim my text briefly. Others will need to read more carefully. The historical background should be useful in understanding the Mormon Faith.
- The third chapter addresses a *very* important question: Which texts should be taken as an authoritative statement of Mormon theology? Where can we find an *official* statement of Mormon theology?
- The fourth chapter provides my understanding of the word *Christian*.
- The fifth through the eighth chapters provide the meat of this booklet: A series of contrasts between Mormon and orthodox Christian theologies.
- The ninth and final chapter provides my personal reflections and conclusions.

---

[1] In general, I will attempt to document the case I'm making in these endnotes at the conclusion of each chapter. In this case, I will intentionally refrain from noting the source of the quotation.

[2] In the text that follows, I will frequently use the word, "orthodox" or "orthodoxy" (lower-case "o"). The consensus theology held by the church since the early centuries has always been called "orthodoxy." Don't confuse orthodoxy with the "Orthodox Churches" (upper-

case "O"). The Orthodox Churches are autonomous national churches in communion with the Patriarch of Constantinople (Istanbul) – Greek Orthodox and Russian Orthodox, for example. The entire Orthodox communion is often called "Eastern Orthodoxy". Catholic and Protestant Christians can be "orthodox," while not participating in the "Eastern Orthodox" community.

[3] See the "Suggested Readings".

[4] The official name of the largest Mormon organization is "The Church of Jesus Christ of Latter-Day Saints," often abbreviated as "LDS." I occasionally use the initials, but only when I'm referring specifically to the organization. More often, I will use the phrase, "the Mormon Faith", to refer to a system of ideas, to a religious perspective. And finally, I refer to members of the LDS church as *Mormons*.

[5] Note the book by that title mentioned in the Suggested Readings.

2. A Brief History of the Mormon Faith

It's impossible to understand the Mormon Faith without some knowledge of Joseph Smith and the origins of the Mormon movement. What follows is, therefore, the briefest of histories. Indeed, the chapter title could just as well have been: The Mormon Faith: A Historical Sketch.

Moreover, it's hard to be a part of our culture without knowing that Mormons are associated with polygamy, golden tablets, visions and angels. It's hard to write about that without being a bit flamboyant! But … in what follows, I'll do my best to avoid that.

I know that Mormons are sometimes embarrassed by their history. I acknowledge that. But my intent in this chapter is simple. It is not to embarrass Mormons, but rather to provide a bit of historical context so that the theological discussion that follows makes some sense. [1]

2.1. Joseph Smith and the Origins of the Mormon Faith

In 1805, Joseph Smith was born into a poor farming family in Vermont. When he was eleven, the family relocated to Palmyra, New York, a small community east of Rochester, NY. We know little remarkable about Smith during his early childhood. However, historians sometimes refer to the area where he was raised as the *Burned-over District* because waves of revivals swept through upper New York State during the period. Smith would have been exposed to camp meetings and revivalists of all sorts.

2.1.1. Smith's Early Revelations

Sometime in the early 1820s, when Smith would have been in his mid-to-late-teens, he claimed to have had his "First Vision." In his vision, Smith met Jesus, who announced his forgiveness and told him that he should avoid all of the existing denominations. Through that vision, Smith learned that "true Christianity" had been lost toward the end of the Apostolic age – about 90 A.D. – and that he was being called to launch the *restoration* of the Church.

Subsequently, he claimed to have had a series of visions brought by various angelic beings. In one of those visions, the Angel Moroni revealed the existence and location of a set of golden plates inscribed in an ancient Egyptian dialect. However, Moroni commanded Smith, not to show the plates to others without explicit permission. When he unearthed them, Smith also discovered the Urim and Thummin, which enabled him to read the texts.

Smith claimed that the plates provided an account of several waves of emigrants from the Old World into the New World. The third wave brought the sons of Nephi, who were eventually decimated in a battle with earlier inhabitants of the land. The final two Nephites were Mormon and his son Moroni (who after his death and resurrection became the Angel Moroni). Before they died, they wrote the history contained on the plates and buried them in upstate New York in A.D. 384.

In late 1827, with the help of his young wife, Smith began the process of translating the texts. In 1830, he completed and published *The Book of Mormon*.

2.1.2. The Origins of the Mormon Movement

During the next 14 years, the "Mormon" movement grew rapidly in spite of intense persecution. The details need not detain us long, but local persecution led the Mormons to relocate on several occasions. The new movement moved from New York to Kirtland, Ohio in 1831. In 1837, Smith's followers again moved west to Missouri. The following year was particularly tumultuous; armed conflicts broke out between Mormons and non-Mormons within the Missouri Territory. Those conflicts, known in retrospect as the *Mormon War*, led Governor Lilburn Boggs to issue *Missouri Executive Order* 44, sometimes called the *Extermination Order*, on October 27, 1838. His order allowed the military to treat Mormons as enemies of the state and to take decisive action against them.[2] That fall, Smith and some of his followers were imprisoned. However, in 1839 the prisoners escaped (or perhaps were allowed to escape) and fled back across the Mississippi River to Nauvoo, Illinois.

During the next few years, Smith continued to receive revelations which exhibited a growing divergence from traditional Christian theology – revelations that continued to fan the fires of persecution. In June 1844, a group of Mormon dissidents founded a press in Nauvoo which attacked the movement. In response, Smith – who was Mayor of Nauvoo at that time – and his followers destroyed the press. In the ensuing conflict, the Illinois militia jailed Smith. Then, on June 27, 1844, a mob attacked the jailhouse. During that attack, Smith and his brother Hyrum were shot and killed.

2.2. The Mormon Faith under the Leadership of Brigham Young

2.2.1. The Succession Crisis

During the years prior to his death, Smith implemented a variety of organizational structures in order to lead the growing Mormon movement, but his plans didn't include a clear plan of succession. Consequently, after his death, it wasn't immediately obvious who should lead the movement. Smith's brother Hyrum, one of the three members of the First Presidency, would have been a candidate, except that he died with Smith. Smith's son Joseph Smith III would have been a possibility, except that he was only eleven at the time. Sidney Rigdon, the surviving member of the First Presidency, could and did make a strong case for leadership. Brigham Young, the President of the Quorum of the Twelve, argued that there could be no true successor to Joseph Smith and that the Quorum of the Twelve should assume leadership.

On August 8, 1844, a conference was held in Nauvoo, IL, to discuss the issue. Rigdon spoke first and made his case for leadership. Afterwards, Young argued his case for the Quorum of the Twelve. The majority favored Young's position. The Quorum of the Twelve, with Young as President, assumed leadership of the movement. Two months later (October 6-7, 1844), the Quorum of the Twelve presided over a General Conference that sustained Young's leadership role.

Some of the other claimants to leadership were not willing to acquiesce to Young's leadership, and several of them formed splinter groups – some of which continue to function today. The details are far too complex to detain us here. But in the end, Smith's son, Joseph Smith III, was asked to lead the largest of the splinter groups, a group which came to be known as the Reorganized Church of Jesus Christ of Latter-day Saints. Today, the group is known as the Community of Christ and is based in Independence, MO.

The group that followed Young, The Church of Jesus Christ of Latter-day Saints, now numbers about 13 million. The Reorganized Church – or the Community of Christ, as they prefer to be called – numbers about 250,000. In addition, there is a handful of splinter groups, each of which numbers less than 40,000.

2.2.2. The Migration to Utah

As noted above, Smith's ideas were simply too radical to be accepted by the general public – which explains why various state and local officials encouraged the Mormons to move on at various times – sometimes violently.

Because of the hostilities against the Mormons in Nauvoo, IL that led to Smith's murder in 1844, Young encouraged the members of the movement to migrate west – beyond the purview of United States law – for their own safety. He planned for them to begin traveling in April 1846. However, that was not to be. In response to on-going threats from the Illinois state militia, the Mormons chose to cross the Mississippi River on short notice in February 1846 and to begin traveling west. They hoped to enter Mexican territory on the far side of Missouri, which they perceived as safer. That fall, they stopped for the winter just north of Omaha, Nebraska. Because they had been forced to leave Nauvoo on short notice, they lacked adequate supplies for such a migration. And as

The Mormon Faith 13

consequence, the winter of 1846-47 was hard, and sickness was common.

During that winter, Young consulted with travelers and trappers. Convinced that the Mormons should migrate to an unpopulated area, he selected the Great Basin in Utah. Early in 1847, Young organized a group to scout the route west, and then, in April 1847, the Mormons continued their migration westward. They arrived at Fort Laramie, Wyoming, on June 1, 1847. After a brief stay, they pushed on, arriving in Fort Bridger, Wyoming on July 7th, and then finally, they reached the Salt Lake Valley on July 24, 1847 – commemorated by the State of Utah as *Pioneer Day*. During the next twenty years about 70,000 Mormons migrated to what came to be known as Salt Lake City.

2.2.3. Brigham Young's "Adam-God Theory"

On April 9, 1852, at the Church's General Conference, Brigham Young proposed what has since been known as the Adam-God Theory or the Adam-God Doctrine. Briefly, he seems to have argued that Adam was the God who created this world, and hence he is the father of us all. However, his formulation contained ambiguities which have hindered subsequent commentators from explicating his ideas precisely. And, from the first, his ideas generated a good deal of controversy.

Controversy notwithstanding, Young continue to preach his ideas during the next twenty-five years. However, after his death in 1877, the church gradually distanced itself from his theories. Finally in 1974, the LDS president Spencer W. Kimball stated, "We denounce [the Adam-God] theory and hope that everyone will be cautioned against this and other kinds of false doctrine."

2.2.4. The Mormon Reformation

All religious movements attract ardent and committed believers. But inevitably, they also attract others who believe casually and some who seem to have little faith at all. The Mormon movement was no exception. And so, in the early 1850s, Mormons began to discuss how to deal with those who were, for all practical purposes, on the fringe.

In 1855, a drought struck the Salt Lake basin area. Some interpreted the drought as God's judgment. Then, as the drought hung on into the following year, preaching became more passionate. With the full and strong support of the First Presidency, some responded with renewed commitment. Moreover, some presented themselves for *rebaptism*, as a symbol of their renewed commitment.

In the midst of the process, some Mormon preachers began to speak of *blood atonement* – the idea that true apostates might have become so enveloped in sin that their own blood might be necessary in order to achieve salvation.

In one of his sermons, Brigham Young stated:

> "I know that there are transgressors, who, if they knew themselves and the only condition upon which they can obtain forgiveness, would beg of their brethren to shed their blood, that the smoke might ascend to God as an offering to appease the wrath that is kindled against them, and that the law might have its course."[3]

The LDS church never approved or advocated Young's idea. I include it here as an indication of the tenor of the

2.3. The Mormon Faith Since Brigham Young

2.3.1. Polygamy within the Mormon Faith

It's hard to know where to put a few paragraphs about polygamy among the Mormons. And yet, I can't ignore the topic. After all, the practice has caused the Mormons no end of grief. In the end, I've chosen to deal with the topic at the point historically where the Mormons repudiated the practice and re-entered the mainstream ... at least on this issue.

Let's begin with a distinction: A *plural marriage* is a marriage between a living man and a living woman, recognized by the church, that creates a polygamous union. A *sealing* in contrast is a union between a man and a woman which will lead to a *celestial marriage* – a marriage after death. Marriages are "until death do us part"; sealings are "for time and eternity". Discussion of marriage among the Mormons can be both convoluted and controversial. When reading the history, one must distinguish between a marriage and a sealing.

Approval for plural marriages seems to have begun with Joseph Smith – although that is debated. There is some evidence that Smith received a revelation that supported the practice of polygamy in 1831. Some historians claim that Smith married a second wife as early as 1833. However, the practice remained highly controversial until 1852, when Brigham Young supported the practice.

Moreover, Brigham Young practiced polygamy – he had twenty wives. During the next few decades, plural marriages remained a Mormon distinctive – and also a practice which kept Utah from obtaining statehood.

Then, in 1890, Wilford Woodruff, the Church's president, received a revelation that declared an end to plural marriages. The decision also cleared the way for Utah to be accepted as a state, which happened in 1896. Following that decision, Mormons gradually merged into the broader American mainstream – albeit still with their distinctives. However, some of the splinter groups have continued to espouse polygamy until the present – a topic I'll return to in a few more paragraphs.

2.3.2. The Role of Afro-Americans within the Mormon Faith

When the Mormon Faith originated in the 1830s, slavery was still legal – not just the possession of slaves, you understand; trafficking in slaves was also legal. In that kind of environment, the roles of Blacks would have naturally been limited. Nonetheless, several Blacks did join the Mormon movement during the early years. They were not, however, allowed to enter the priesthood. And that remained the official Mormon position until 1978, when President Spencer W. Kimball announced his reception of a revelation which allowed Blacks to enter the priesthood. Since then, Blacks have been able to participate fully in the Mormon Faith.

2.3.3. Mormon Fundamentalism

As noted above, Smith's death in 1844 led to a succession crisis and eventually to the formation of some splinter groups. It's important to note in this brief historical sketch

The Mormon Faith

that some of those splinter groups continue to exist. Moreover, some of them continue to insist that their faith allows for – indeed encourages – polygamy.

As noted just above, the mainstream of the Mormon movement has not taught or sanctioned polygamy for over a hundred years. Nonetheless, the secular media seems to be fascinated with Mormon Fundamentalism and occasionally highlights them because of their on-going commitment to polygamy.

---

[1] For a brief introduction to Joseph Smith and the Mormon faith, see the following: Robert L. Millet, *The Mormon Faith: A New Look at Christianity*; Robert L. Millet, "Introduction: How it all began," in *A Different Jesus? The Christ of the Latter-day Saints*; and *Building the Kingdom: a History of Mormons in America* by Claudia Lauper Bushman and Richard Lyman Bushman.

[2] Details about the Mormon War and the Extermination Order can be found on the web pages of the Missouri Secretary of State: www.sos.mo.gov/archives/resources/mormon.asp. The order states that "… the Mormons must be treated as enemies, and must be exterminated or driven from the State if necessary for the public peace – their outrages are beyond all description." The order was officially rescinded on June 25, 1976.

[3] *Journal of Discourses* 4:53-54. The *Journal of Discourses* is a collection of Mormon sermons from the mid-1850s to the late 1880s. The LDS leadership acknowledges that the sermons provide interesting evidence for understanding the period, but they insist that the sermons – including those of Brigham Young himself – are not authoritative.

3. Sources of Mormon Theology

Mormon theologians base their theology on a set of documents they call "The Standard Works of the Church" (that is, the King James translation of *The Bible*, *The Book of Mormon*, *The Pearl of Great Price*, and *The Doctrine and Covenants*)[1] "… as interpreted by the general authorities of the Church – the current apostles and prophets."[2] That statement calls for two observations.

First of all, I find it very odd that Mormons base their theology on an English translation of the Greek text rather than on the Greek text itself. The Apostle Paul, for example, wrote his letters in *Koine Greek*. From the earliest centuries, Christians have held his letters to be inspired scripture and translations to be just that – translations. It is true that Mormons commonly qualify their commitment to the King James Version by the words "…as far as it is translated correctly."[3] However, they continue to publish and use the King James translation.

I'll be honest; that doesn't make much sense to me. However, I'm not going to make a fuss about the issue. The contrasts I want to make in the chapters that follow can be made equally well from the 17th century King James Translation of *The Bible* or a 21st century translation.

Second, it's hard to get a handle on Mormon theology because it is, to some extent, a moving target. The phrase "as interpreted by …" reflects that difficulty and the inherent ambiguity in writing about Mormon theology.[4] Joseph Smith claimed to be a prophet, and he acknowledged that other prophets would follow him. And hence, the Mormon Church continues to believe in on-going revelation.

Chapter 10 of *Gospel Principles*, an official publication of the LDS church, is devoted to the Mormon understanding of Scripture. It states their position as follows:

> "The Church of Jesus Christ of Latter-day Saints accepts four books as scripture: The Bible, the Book of Mormon, the Doctrine and the Covenants and the Pearl of Great Price. These books are called the standard works of the Church. The inspired words of our living prophets are also accepted as scripture."[5]

Later in the chapter, we learn:

> "In addition to these four books of scripture, the inspired words of our living prophets become scripture to us. Their words come to us through conferences, the *Liahona* or *Ensign* magazine, and instructions to local priesthood leaders."[6]

Based on these texts, I would conclude that official publications of the First Presidency should be taken as official statements of the Mormon Faith.

However, to be fair, I need to note the following qualification: The Mormon Church considers the person holding the office of President of the Mormon Church to be a prophet, and hence capable of speaking authoritatively. However, The Mormon Church does not claim that *all* words spoken by any one of the various Presidents are inspired, and that includes the founder himself, Joseph Smith. The holder of that office must *intend* to speak with authority. Given that, the status of Smith's sermons is unclear. Let's look at just one specific example.

Just a few months prior to his death in 1844, Smith gave a funeral oration for a man with the unusual name of King Follett. The document which reports that oration is normally entitled "The King Follett Discourse." In that discourse, Smith indicated clearly and unequivocally that he was providing his understanding of Mormon theology. But that raises the question: Should outsiders use this Discourse as an authoritative statement of Mormon theology. A "No" would seem to undermine the status of Smith, the founding prophet of the church. After all, if he didn't understand Mormon theology a few months before his death, perhaps no one does. On the other hand, a "Yes" would expand the list of authoritative documents. And I understand fully why Mormon theologians try to avoid the horns of this dilemma. He taught some ideas in the *Discourse* which some Mormons would prefer to forget.[7]

The way the church dealt with Brigham Young's Adam-God Doctrine provides an interesting parallel case. As I noted in the previous chapter, Brigham Young, the second prophet of the church, held and advocated a theological position known as the *Adam-God Theory*. During his lifetime, some agreed with him; some did not. After his death, his theory provoked a good deal of dissension. Eventually, in 1976, Spencer W. Kimball, the twelfth President of the Mormon Church, denounced the doctrine. To suggest today that the Mormon Church holds the doctrine would be irresponsible in the light of their official repudiation of it. In contrast, the Mormon Church has not repudiated any of Smith's teachings. And so, it seems reasonable to treat Smith as a competent *commentator* on Mormon theology – even if we should not treat his sermons as *inspired*.

In 1938, Joseph Fielding Smith, Jr., (The 10th President of the Church) compiled *Teachings of the Prophet Joseph Smith*,[8] a collection of Smith's writings and sermons. And yes, the book includes "The King Follett Discourse." As a President of the Mormon Church, he was considered to be a Mormon prophet, although he didn't claim that his document was inspired. Nonetheless, he seems to have believed that the entire document should be considered authoritative since it all came from the founder of the movement. Again, should we consider the document authoritative?

I've included some background information in the last page or so to help you understand my conundrum. In order to write this booklet, I've had to make a decision about which documents to use as sources for my work. My conclusions are as follows: I have chosen to use the Standard Works; that was an obvious decision. Secondly, I've also chosen to treat any official publication of the First Presidency as an official statement of the LDS Church. Thirdly, I've chosen to use some passages from *Teachings of the Prophet Joseph Smith*.

My third point calls for some explanation. The Mormon Church doesn't consider "The King Follett Discourse" to be inspired. Fair enough. The Mormon Church has the right to make such a judgment. I'll accept their judgment without further discussion. So why am I willing to quote from that discourse? Allow me to present three reasons.

First, it seems to me reasonable to assume that Joseph Smith understood Mormon theology, that he would have been a reasonable *commentator* on Mormon theology – even if a particular discourse or sermon was *not, in fact, inspired*. And hence, I'm willing to quote from "The King Follett Discourse," as well as other writings included in

Teachings of the Prophet Joseph Smith, particularly from the months just prior to his untimely death.

Secondly, Mormon theologians do not agree on this matter. For example, I have used *Mormon Doctrine* by Bruce R. McConkie in the preparation of this booklet. It's a large reference book – over 800 pages – and has been in print for over 40 years. McConkie was a member of the *Quorum of the Twelve*, the most authoritative representatives of the Mormon movement, other than the First Presidency itself. He quotes from *Teachings of the Prophet Joseph Smith* extensively in his exposition of the Mormon Faith. I have also used *We Believe: Doctrines and Principles of the Church of Jesus Christ of Latter-day Saints* by Rulon T. Burton. It too is a large reference book – just short of 1200 pages. In the introduction to his book, Burton explains carefully which sources he quotes, and he makes it absolutely clear that he intends to quote only from authoritative sources. He too quotes extensively from *Teachings of the Prophet Joseph Smith*.

Third, the LDS church seems to accept Smith's sermons as authoritative! *Gospel Principles* is an official publication of the LDS church, intended for education and training within LDS congregations. It quotes from "The King Follett Discourse."[9] If the LDS church is willing to quote from Smith's sermon, then it seems appropriate to accept that sermon as a reasonable statement of LDS theology – even if it is not inspired.

OK, I'll admit it. My decision to quote from some of Smith's sermons will upset some Mormon theologians. The problem is quite simple: Smith taught a range of ideas, some of which are not contained in the Standard Works. For most Mormons, that is not a problem. They simply accept Smith's ideas, since he was the Founding

The Mormon Faith

Prophet of the Mormon Faith. On the other hand, some Mormon theologians are – well, it's hard to put this politely – embarrassed by some of Smith's ideas. Hence, they stress the importance of limiting official Mormon theology to ideas contained in the Standard Works. In the end, the Mormon Church and its theologians will have to sort this out.

The Mormon Church could officially repudiate the teachings of Joseph Smith that cannot be found in the Standard Works. As I noted above, there is precedent for such a decision. The Church officially repudiated Brigham Young's *Adam-God Theory*, and he was the second President of the Church. I've respected that decision. Yes, I mentioned the theory in my thumb-nail historical sketch above because it seemed appropriate to do so. But I don't quote the theory in the chapters on theology that follow; I accept the fact that this doctrine is no longer accepted by the LDS church.

In the meantime, the Church has not repudiated any of the teachings of Joseph Smith. Moreover, the Mormon Church continues to teach ideas taught by Smith that cannot be found in the Standard Works. Given that, I don't see a problem with quoting Smith as an authoritative commentator on the faith – just as some of the Church's theologians do – and just as some of their official publications do.

In other words, the Mormon Church needs to make up its collective mind. Was Joseph Smith, the Founding Prophet, a reliable source of information about Mormon theology … or not? Until the Mormon Church teaches otherwise, I'll treat Joseph Smith's sermons as a reasonable statement of the Mormon Faith.

[1] *The Book of Mormon* is normally published together with *Doctrine and Covenants* and *Pearl of Great Price*, two other works Mormons consider inspired. The three documents are widely available.

[2] Craig L. Blomberg & Stephen E. Robinson, *How Wide the Divide?*, p. 15. Regarding the role of the *Standard Works*, see also:; "Scripture and the Expanding Canon,", Ch. 2 in Millet, *The Mormon Faith*; "The Standard Works" in Bruce R. McConkie, *Mormon Doctrine*; Rulon T. Burton, *We Believe*, pp 917-18; *Gospel Principles*, pp. 45-46; Stephen E. Robinson, *Are Mormons Christians?*, pp. 14-18. Robinson offers an interesting and very extensive discussion of this issue.

[3] Article 8 of "The Articles of Faith of The Church of Jesus Christ of Latter-day Saints" as quoted in *Articles of Faith* by James E. Talmage.

[4] Stephan Robinson is quite candid in this respect. " … we have no professional clergy, no creeds or catechisms, and no theologians in the strict sense. Pure LDS orthodoxy can be a moving target, depending on which Mormon one talks to." Blomberg & Robinson, *How Wide the Divide?* p. 14.

[5] *Gospel Principles*, Chapter 10.

[6] *Liahona* and *Ensign* are both LDS magazines.

[7] For example, Stephen E. Robinson and Robert L. Millet clearly want to speak for the Mormon Faith, and yet – equally clearly – they try to distance themselves from some of the theological positions taken by Joseph Smith toward the end of this life.

[8] *Teachings of the Prophet Joseph Smith* selected and arranged by Joseph Fielding Smith.

[9] *Gospel Principles*, 279

4. Defining the Word *Christian*

Since a study of this sort could easily get out of hand and go on indefinitely, I need to limit my scope. Let me do so by raising a question. Does the Christian Faith have a conceptual or theological core by which it can be defined?

Let me pose a simple mental exercise. Reflect briefly on Mother Teresa and Osama bin Laden. Both of them chose to devote their lives to expressing and implementing religious ideas. Clearly the ideas that motivated them are different, as were their lifestyles. Moreover, even though I'm a Protestant Christian, I resonate with Mother Teresa (a Catholic) and I do not resonate with Osama bin Laden (a Muslim). Why? It seems obvious to me that I share some fundamental theological ideas with Mother Teresa that Osama bin Laden would reject. And those ideas lead to different lifestyles. Is that obvious? Surely it is.

But why do I resonate with Mother Teresa when I'm a Protestant and she was a Catholic? After all, she honored the Virgin Mary and the Pope in ways that I consider inappropriate. She and I would have disagreed about the nature and the role of the Sacraments. I could go on, and yet – I acknowledge that we share something fundamentally important. What is it?

Based on these reflections, I would suggest that there is a theological, cognitive core of the Christian faith which defines Christianity, a core that unites all Christians. And Mother Teresa and I would share a commitment to that theological core of the faith, even though we might well disagree over less important issues. In short, Christianity has an *inside* and an *outside*. Christianity is not a Rorschach drawing that individuals may interpret as they please. There are boundaries of the faith. The Apostle Paul was right! There are ideas beyond those boundaries that conflict fundamentally with the "faith once given."

OK, I acknowledge that the boundary itself is fuzzy. There is some ambiguity. But that won't be a problem in the pages that follow. I don't intend to define the boundary precisely. Rather I want to explore the theological center, the ideas the church has confessed again and again.

C. S. Lewis once offered the suggestion that becoming a Christian is like entering the front door of an old English home. Before you, as the door opens, you see a long entrance hall with rooms off both sides. No one in his right mind would remain and live in the entrance hall. All of the proper *living* occurs in the rooms off the entrance hall.[1]

In context, Lewis was suggesting that one cannot live in the entrance hall of Christianity. One must make a choice and worship, for example, as an Anglican or as a Baptist or as a Methodist. Let's accept that as a given. His metaphor makes a good point. But it also raises a tacit question about the *organizational rooms* one might find off the Christian *entrance hall*. It seems reasonable – at least to me for the reasons I've been suggesting – to acknowledge that there is a Catholic room and a Baptist room. But is there a Jehovah's Witnesses room or a room for those of the Mormon Faith, for example? Or to ask the question more directly, are those two groups expressions of Christianity or not? Both of them claim to be. Are they? How about the Unitarian Universalist Association? The Association has historic roots in the Protestant Reformation. But several centuries ago the Unitarians repudiated Trinitarian theology, and over time, Unitarians ceased to think of themselves as Christians. Today, many – perhaps most – members of the Association would disclaim the label *Christian*. So, where do they fit in? Or do they?

I'm asking, then, How inclusive is the Christian Faith? Is it possible to define the word *Christian*? In order to think about that question, we'll need a conceptual model that will provide some guidance.

The diagram that follows provides my answer to the question of how to draw the boundary of the Christian Faith. By implication, it demonstrates how I use the word *Christian*. The theological core of the Christian faith sets forth three theological affirmations: affirmations about God, affirmations about the person and work of Jesus Christ, and affirmations about the nature of our humanity. Note that all of the core affirmations are ontological.

Ontology

The word *ontology* is built from the Greek word *ontos*, which means *being*. So, ontology is the study of *being*. It asks, What is real? What is the nature of reality? Theists hold that God is real. That's an ontological assertion. Atheists deny that God exists. That too is an ontological assertion – albeit, a negative one. Theologians ask ontological questions like, What does it mean to be a human being? In the first few centuries after the church was founded, theologians agreed that Jesus Christ was both God and man, but they found it difficult to speak about that ontological reality in a coherent and persuasive way. Their theological reflections were, therefore, attempts to speak about that reality.

Thinking about the Core of the Christian Faith

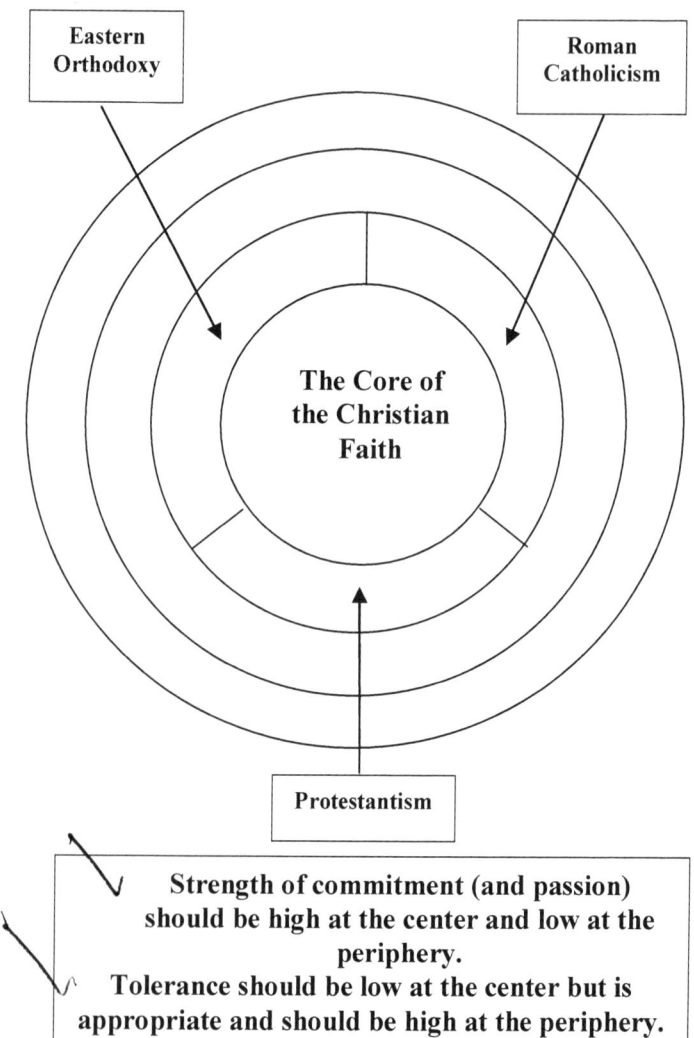

The Mormon Faith

The Core of the Christian Faith:

The essential doctrines of the faith: God, the Trinity, Christ (both His person and work) and our Humanity as defined by the early church in the 4th & 5th centuries.

The Inner Ring:

Three major branches of the faith with three approaches to the Doctrines of:
the Bible, Authority and Subjective Soteriology (How individuals receive the gift of salvation).
These doctrinal issues split the church in the 11th Century and again during the 16th Century Reformation.

The Middle Ring:

Doctrines that require a decision about how to lead the church – and so tend to split churches: Doctrines of Ecclesiology (Church government, baptism and the Lord's Supper), the use of the Gifts of the Spirit in the church service

The Outer Ring:

Minor doctrines and ideas where tolerance is appropriate and Christians can agree to disagree: Predestination-Free Will; Eschatology (Prophecy and the End Times); political implications of the Christian Faith

The church established the theological core of the Christian faith during the first five centuries after the death of the Apostles – roughly between 100 and 600 A.D. The core of the faith comprises those doctrines shared by Christians around the world, Protestant, Catholic, and Orthodox. It seems to me that a commitment to those core theological ideas constitutes a minimum standard for being considered Christian.

Stephen Robinson, a Mormon theologian, wrote a book with the provocative title, *Are Mormons Christians?*[2] In his book, he argues that it is impossible to define the word *Christian* successfully. Each of the chapters in his book examines a traditional strategy for defining *Christian*. He suggests that each of the strategies is flawed. For example, narrow definitions tacitly exclude early Christians. After all, prior to the Council of Nicea in 325 A.D. when the Church defined and adopted the doctrine of the trinity it would have been impossible to believe in the doctrine of the trinity. So, if belief in the doctrine of the trinity is essential to being a Christian, then there were no true Christians prior to that Council.

Robinson acknowledges that historians have traditionally thought of the Christian Faith as having three major branches: Orthodox, Catholic, and Protestant. And he acknowledges that the Mormon Faith is not included within any one of those three major branches. He suggests, therefore, that the Mormon Faith is a new form of Christianity and claims that the Mormon Faith has as much right to be considered *Christian* as the three more traditional branches.

In my opinion, his approach is flawed. Many and perhaps most of the metaphors for the Church in the New Testament were organic: Jesus claimed to be the true vine and the head of the body. I would suggest that it's helpful to think organically, to think of the church as a large tree. A tree trunk supports an entire tree. Every little twig is connected to a branch and ultimately supported by the trunk.

During the first few centuries, the entire church working together developed a range of theological ideas that I am calling *the core of the faith*. Today, the church worldwide continues to teach those ideas. That core supports the theology of the church much the way a trunk supports a tree.

Over time, the Church did lose its organizational unity – first, when the East and the West split in the 11th century and later on in the 16th century when Roman Catholics and Protestants split again. After those splits, the three major branches of the Christian Faith differed theologically. In fact, they differed decisively! And so, Robinson is logically correct at one point. The three major branches of traditional Christianity – and all of the thousands of Protestant denominations – have distinctive approaches to theology. And if those distinctives are used to define the Christian Faith, then there is no common denominator.

But, if you think about the Christian Faith organically, Robinson's problem disappears. Let me explain. I happen to be an Evangelical Christian. As such, my theology differs in very important ways from Roman Catholic theology. But Evangelicals and Catholics claim to be descended from the early Church. And yes, we all acknowledge that our lineage runs through the Council of Nicea. As my metaphor indicates, Evangelicals and Catholics are supported by the same trunk. We share a common commitment to the theological core of the Christian faith as indicated by the diagram.

The Mormon Faith, in contrast, does not share that commitment. Refer again to the historical chapter of this document. Joseph Smith's account of his first vision indicated that God told him explicitly that the church had fallen away from the truth during the late part of the 1st century – a Mormon doctrine known as *The Great Apostasy*. The Church, according to Smith, wandered in confusion for over 1,700 years, until God appointed him as a prophet and charged him with *restoring* the true church. He claimed, in short, that the Mormon Faith is rooted in Jesus Christ, but he denied that the Mormon Faith shares the historic lineage which I described metaphorically as the trunk of a tree.

Mormons deny any participation in the Christian heritage, and yet they want to be called *Christian*. That makes no sense to me. Suggesting that the Mormon Faith, which repudiates that heritage, is Christian makes about as much sense as talking about a tree limb that is not supported by a tree trunk.

It's tempting to throw in the towel at this point and admit that the theological gulf between Christians and Mormons is insurmountable. And yet, I think there is more to be said. Even if Christians and Mormons disagree about whether the Church fell away from the truth – which they do – we can jointly agree to limit our discussion to the ideas that I have proposed as the core of the faith. Doing so will keep this discussion from becoming absolutely interminable. Moreover, it will allow orthodox Christians and Mormons to understand their differences. And those are goals worth pursuing.

In the four chapters that follow, we'll get to the heart of the matter. I'll compare and contrast Mormon and

Christian theology. As I said in the Introduction, I don't intend to defend Christian theology, nor do I intend to attack Mormon theology. That's not the point. Rather, I'll place the two perspectives in parallel without much comment; the contrasts should speak for themselves. I'll hold my personal reflections for the final chapter.[3]

---

[1] See the "Preface" to C. S. Lewis, *Mere Christianity*.

[2] Stephen E. Robinson. *Are Mormons Christians?*.

[3] Robinson provides a brief, but very useful statement of the Mormon faith in *How Wide the Divide?* pp. 16-18. He acknowledges specifically that ontological issues separate the Mormon faith from orthodox Christianity. For a more thorough account, refer to *Mormon Doctrine* by Bruce R. McConkie and *We Believe*, ed. by Rulon T. Burton. *A Study of the Articles of Faith* by James E. Talmage was written over a hundred years ago and is considered a classic statement of Mormon theology.

5. God and His Universe

5.1. God, as the Creator

God called Abraham, while he still lived in Ur of the Chaldees, to leave his home for a land that God promised to show him. At that time, Abraham was probably a polytheist. He agreed to follow God, and God *alone*, but there is nothing in the Old Testament text to indicate that Abraham understood the idea that there really were no other gods. It took God hundreds of years to help Abraham's descendents understand that He – and He ALONE – was God, and that there really were no other gods. By about 800 B.C. or perhaps 700, some of Abraham's descendents had grasped the concept of monotheism – but NOT by any means all of them! It took hundreds of additional years before the Jewish people as a whole grasped and adopted monotheism.

Somewhere in that long process, Abraham's descendents came to understand another basic concept, a concept that is really a corollary of the first idea: <u>If there is only one God, and if he – and he alone – has existed eternally, then he was the creator of all that exists.</u>

At the time Jesus was born, the Jewish people would have assumed that perspective – without giving it much thought. Jesus spoke often about God, but always from within that framework. He did introduce some new ideas. For example, he taught us to call God "Abba," that is "Daddy." In so doing, he made God much more accessible. But he didn't focus specifically on monotheism or on God as the Creator. He seems to have taken those ideas for granted.

Moreover, Jesus assumed that God was Spirit, distinct from this universe. When he was speaking to the Samaritan woman (John 4), he said that "God is Spirit, so those who worship him must worship in spirit and in truth."

A century after Jesus' life, and long after the last of the apostles had died, several Christian theologians grasped another corollary of the ideas they had inherited from the Jewish people: if God alone existed from eternity, and if God created all that is, then he must have created *ex nihilo* – out of nothing. The Bible doesn't say explicitly that God created *ex nihilo*. But that conclusion does seem to follow from the idea of God as the creator of all that exists. Christians have maintained that perspective almost unanimously since the second century.

In the 19th century, the philosopher/theologian Soren Kierkegaard offered the following formulation: there is "an infinite and qualitative difference between God and man". The expression was new; the idea wasn't. After all, if God is eternal, and beyond space and time, as most Christians believe, and if we humans are mortal, spatial and temporal, then Kierkegaard's statement would seem to follow. Saying all of this yet another way, contemporary orthodox Christian theologians often speak of a fundamental distinction between the Creator and the creation.

The Mormon Faith differs from this traditional perspective in three distinct ways.

First of all, Joseph Smith held that everything which has existence is material; there is no *immaterial* or *spiritual* existence.

> "There is no such thing as immaterial matter. All spirit is matter, but it is more fine or pure, and can only be discerned by purer eyes; We cannot see it; but when our bodies are purified we shall see that it is all matter."[1]

Smith, in short, was a materialist.

Now I must admit that I'm sorely tempted to take a long digression at this point. Smith's position has some striking similarities to the ideas of the Epicurean and Stoic philosophers that Paul met *and opposed* on the Areopagus. (Acts 17). But I'll resist the temptation for now and simply note the similarity.

Second, Smith denied that God created the heavens and the earth. He held that matter is co-eternal with God. God is, therefore, a craftsman but not a creator – at least not a creator as the Church has understood the term. Smith stated his perspective in many places, but The King Follett Discourse expresses his ideas most clearly.

> "Now, the word create came from the [Hebrew word] *baurau* (sic) which does not mean to create out of nothing; it means to organize; the same as a man would organize materials and build a ship. Hence, we infer that God had materials to organize the world out of chaos – chaotic matter, which is element, and in which dwells all the glory. Element had an existence from the time he had. The pure principles of element are principles which can never be destroyed; they may be organized and re-organized, but not destroyed. They had no beginning, and can have no end."[2]

Again, I'll note the similarity with Greek philosophy. The Greek philosopher Aristotle – like Smith – held that God was a craftsman, but not a creator.

And thirdly, Mormon theology does not acknowledge a fundamental distinction between God and humanity or a fundamental distinction between the Creator and the creation. Mormon theologians sometimes say explicitly that God the Father and human beings are *of the same species*.[3]

Moreover, Mormons speak of salvation as *deification*.[4] Now while most Protestants will find the idea of *deification* new and rather strange, the term is, in fact, not new. Greek speaking theologians have used the term since the second century. However, prior to Joseph Smith, no one had ever used the term to assert that all Christians will become gods – literally – which is exactly what Smith asserted in "The King Follett Discourse." At the resurrection, he claimed, we will:

> "... inherit the same power, the same glory and
> the same exaltation, until you arrive at the station
> of a God, and ascend the throne of eternal power,
> the same as those who have gone before."[5]

I'll focus on the Mormon doctrine of deification in more detail in chapter 8.

5.2. God, as Father, Son, and Holy Spirit

This chapter is not about Jesus of Nazareth; we'll focus on Jesus of Nazareth as the incarnate God/Man in chapter 7. This chapter is about God. But Jesus of Nazareth, by his very existence as a human being, forced people in the first century (just as he forces us today!) to respond to the question: What kind of God do we worship? How is it possible for the sovereign God of the entire universe to become a human being?

All human theorizing emerges when we come face to face with something profoundly puzzling. Theology is simply one case in point. In this case, the puzzle is this: Jesus' Disciples, before they met him, were expecting a Messiah – probably a political Messiah – someone who would kick the Romans out of Palestine. After they had become Disciples, they discovered that Jesus was much more than they had expected, indeed different from what they had expected. As they followed Jesus, his words and behavior presented them with the ultimate paradox. On the one hand, he was clearly a human being – he wasn't some kind of ethereal mirage. As he walked and talked with them, he got tired, he got thirsty, and he got hungry. On the other hand, he exercised extraordinary powers: he cast out demons; he healed the sick; he even raised the dead! Furthermore, he claimed to be able to forgive sins – surely God's prerogative! Toward the end of his public ministry, he claimed to be one with the heavenly Father.

That's the problem they faced: Jesus, their teacher and their friend, seemed to believe that he was God – God, just walking around in our world like doing so was nothing special. Moreover, he presented some fairly impressive credentials to back up his claim.

In our experience, only a human nut case would make claims like that. C. S. Lewis, in one of his most quoted passages, articulated the dilemma the Disciples faced as follows:

> "A man who was merely a man and said the sort of things Jesus said would not be a great moral

teacher. He would either be a lunatic - on the level with a man who says he is a poached egg - or he would be the devil of hell. You must take your choice. Either this was, and is, the Son of God, or else a madman or something worse. You can shut Him up for a fool or you can fall at His feet and call Him Lord and God. But let us not come with any patronizing nonsense about His being a great human teacher. He has not left that open to us."[6]

Toward the end of the 4th century, after reflecting about 300 years on questions of this kind, the early church fathers concluded the following:[7]

1) There is only one God. He is the God who manifested himself to the Hebrew people in the Old Testament. In the New Testament Jesus referred to him as "the Father."

2) But, God, the One and Only God, is inherently and eternally complex in ways that transcend our experience, our understanding and our imagination. In a way that we cannot fathom, God is triune. That is, his very nature, his eternal essence, has a three-fold character. Christians confess that when God reveals that three-fold character to us, we meet the Father, the Son and the Holy Spirit. The Father is God, the Son is God, and the Holy Spirit is God. And yet, that inherent three-ness does not in any way compromise the inherent unity or the simplicity of God.

The church eventually developed an elaborate set of linguistic conventions to talk about this triune nature: For example, the creeds say that the Son was eternally *begotten* by the Father, *begotten* and not *made* – that is, not *created*. The Spirit *proceeds* from the Father through the Son – or, if your ancestral roots are in Western Europe

– the Spirit *proceeds* from the Father *and the Son*. But that very way of talking about God raised yet more problems.

Greek and Roman mythology is full of references to the sexual escapades of the various gods and goddesses. And hence, the church had to explain that the word *begat* as used in Christian theology was not in any way sexual. The Father begat the Son eternally; the very being of the Son finds its source in the Father. And that begetting was not sexual, as pagan listeners might have thought. Moreover, the divine Son, the Logos, became a human being in the incarnation. And that *conceiving* by the Holy Spirit was not sexual either.

So, in short, the doctrine of the trinity, as propounded by the early church, was a solution to a problem. It provided a theological foundation for responding to the question: How could Jesus of Nazareth experience fatigue as a human being and yet claim to be one with the heavenly Father, God Himself.

The Mormon Faith differs from this traditional expression in two distinct ways:

First, Mormon theology implicitly denies monotheism. For example, Joseph Smith preached a sermon entitled, "Plurality of Gods."[8] In the introduction to that sermon, Smith stated:

> "I will preach on the plurality of Gods. ... I wish to declare I have always and in all congregations when I have preached on the subject of the Deity, it has been the plurality of Gods. It has been preached by the Elders for fifteen years. I have always declared God to be a distinct personage, Jesus Christ a separate and distinct personage

from God the Father, and that the Holy Ghost was a distinct personage and a Spirit: and these three constitute three distinct personages and three Gods."

Mormon theologians would dispute my interpretation vigorously. They would insist that the previous quotation is consistent with their commitment to monotheism. I must confess, however, that I don't understand that. If Smith's statement isn't polytheism, then I don't know what would qualify as polytheism.

Second, Mormons reject the orthodox doctrine of the trinity. In its place, they teach a doctrine of the *Godhead*. The Godhead, they claim, consists of three "personages," the Father, the Son and the Holy Spirit.[9] Mormons use the three traditional names. However, they explicitly deny the idea that the three personages share some kind of a fundamental "being". The members of the Godhead, they assert, are united solely in purpose. And, as I noted above, Joseph Smith spoke of God in the plural, "the gods." Bruce R. McConkie, a member of the Quorum of the Twelve – the highest ranking body in the Mormon Church – likewise speaks of God in the plural. He summarized the Mormon doctrine of the Godhead this way:

> "We learn these truths relative to the Gods we worship: 1. They are three in number, three separate persons: The first is the Father, the second, the Son; and the third, the Holy Ghost. They are three individuals who meet together, counsel in concert, and as occasion requires travel separately through all immensity. They are three holy men, two having bodies of flesh and bones, the third being a personage of spirit."[10]

To orthodox Christians, that certainly appears to be Tri-Theism.

5.3. God, as Father

As I noted above, orthodox Christianity has always taught that the triune God is spiritual and not material. It's true, as I'll note below; God the Son did take on our humanity, including our physical nature. However, God, as God, is spiritual. And more specifically, God the Father is spiritual and does not participate in our physical nature.

<u>In contrast, Joseph Smith taught that God the Father is an exalted human being.</u>

> "God himself was once as we are now, and is an exalted man, and sits enthroned in yonder heavens! ... We have imagined and supposed that God was God from all eternity. I will refute that idea, and take away the veil, so that you may see. ... It is the first principle of the Gospel to know for a certainty the Character of God, and to know that we may converse with him as one man converses with another, and that he was once a man like us; yea, that God himself, the Father of us all, dwelt on an earth, the same as Jesus Christ himself did ..."[11]

We'll come back to the idea of *exaltation* below. It's a key concept in Mormon theology. For now, I simply want to emphasize that the Mormon Faith teaches clearly that God the Father, as an exalted human being, continues to exist as an embodied being, that God the Father has flesh and blood, just as all other humans do.[12]

Moreover, Mormons hold that God the Father, as an exalted human being, must have had a father, just as we do.[13] The Standard Works, which Mormons hold to be authoritative, provide no account whatsoever about the origins of the man who became God the Father. However, Joseph Smith clearly believed that God the Father also had a Father.[14]

Mormon theology expands on God's *Fatherhood* in two additional ways:
- Mormons hold that God the Father (together with the Divine Mother) is the father of the entire human race.
- Mormons hold that God the Father is physically the father of Jesus Christ.

We'll come back to each of these points in the two chapters that follow.

5.4. Conclusion

At this point it should be clear that the orthodox Christian and the Mormon understanding of the nature of God, of God's Fatherhood, and of the creation itself and are in fundamental conflict.

---

[1] *Doctrine and Covenants*, 131:7-8

[2] See "The King Follett Discourse" in Joseph Fielding Smith, *Teachings of the Prophet Joseph Smith*, pp. 350 – 53. *Gospel Principles* does not emphasize the point. However, when discussing creation, the LDS official statement indicates that God "organized this world and gave it form, motion and life," p. 5.

[3] See Millet, *A Different Jesus?,* p. 117 and Robert L. Millet and Gregory C. V. Johnson, *Bridging the Divide*, p. 58. Richard J. Mouw, President of Fuller Theological

Seminary, wrote an "Afterward" for *A Different Jesus*. In the "Afterward," Mouw made it absolutely clear that the Mormon commitment to talking of God and humanity as "of the same species" was absolutely unacceptable to him theologically. He wrote gently, but in the end, he was clear that the difference between Mormon theology and orthodox theology was a difference of "worldview." There is an irreconcilable theological conflict between the two.

[4] Blomberg & Robinson, *How Wide the Divide?*, pp. 80-87 and Millet, *A Different Jesus?*, pp. 116-18.

[5] Joseph Fielding Smith, *Teachings of the Prophet Joseph Smith*, p. 347. In *Doctrine and Covenants* 132:15-20, Joseph Smith discussed various forms of marriage. In that context, he declared that those who were married in the church would be exalted. Moreover, "Then shall they be gods, because they have no end; therefore shall they be from everlasting to everlasting, because they continue; then shall they be above all, because all things are subject unto them. Then shall they be gods, because they have all power, and the angels are subject unto them."

[6] C. S. Lewis, *Mere Christianity*, Bk. II, Ch 3.

[7] The core of what follows was established at the Council of Nicea in 325 A.D. However, the church continued to work out some of the details over the next several hundred years. For those interested in more information, *Early Christian Doctrine* by Kelly remains the definitive text.

[8] "Sermon by the Prophet – The Christian Godhead – Plurality of Gods, Meeting in the Grove, east of the Temple, June 16, 1844," Joseph Fielding Smith, *Teachings of the Prophet Joseph Smith*, pp. 369-76. The sermon is sometimes called the "Sermon in the Grove" and sometimes "Plurality of Gods." As I acknowledged above, this sermon is not part of the "standard works," and hence should not be considered as authoritative in defining Mormon theology. It does, however, reflect Joseph

Smith's understanding of Mormon theology shortly before his death.

[9] See "Godhead" in McConkie, *Mormon Doctrine*, for a concise statement of Mormon theology. Burton, *We Believe*, pp. 352-57, provides extensive quotations on the subject.

[10] Quoted in "Doctrine 289" in Burton, *We Believe*, pp. 353-355.

[11] "The King Follett Discourse" in Joseph Fielding Smith, *Teachings of the Prophet Joseph Smith*, pp. 345-46.

[12] See *Doctrine and Covenants*, 130:22; Bruce McConkie, *Mormon Doctrine*, p. 250; *Gospel Principles*, p. 6.

[13] Joseph Smith expounded extensively on this subject in the "King Follett Discourse." See Joseph Fielding Smith, *Teachings of the Prophet Joseph Smith*, pp. 345-46.

[14] "Plurality of Gods," Joseph Fielding Smith, *Teaching of the Prophet Joseph Smith*, p. 373. Was there an infinite regress? Perhaps. Smith wasn't clear on the matter.

6. Humanity: Origins and Fall

The study of theology normally moves from a discussion about the nature of God to a discussion about the nature of Jesus Christ. However, the structure of Mormon theology suggests a different order. I need to address the subject of our origins and the fall of man first. Those ideas will provide the foundation for thinking about Jesus Christ in the following chapter.

6.1. Origins

The Bible speaks of human origins in the first few chapters of Genesis. The story is quite simple. I'm sure you know the story of Adam and Eve. The key verses are found in Genesis 1:27 and 2:7 (New Living Translation):

> "So God created people in his own image; God patterned them after himself; male and female he created them."

> "And the Lord God formed a man's body from the dust of the ground and breathed into it the breath of life. And the man became a living person."

As I said, the story itself is really quite simple. Yes, theologians have written a great deal about the nature of the "image of God" but the story fills only a few verses.

The Mormon account, in contrast, is extraordinarily complex.

The Mormon Faith

In the section above (5.1.), I noted Smith's materialism – his doctrine that all that exists is material. However, I omitted an interesting detail that I'll need to clarify in this context. Joseph Smith taught that there are two kinds of matter: 1) *Element*, the raw matter from which God the Father formed the physical universe, and 2) *Spirit* (sometimes called *Intelligence*), a second kind of matter and the raw material from which God formed his Spirit-Children. Spirit is a fine form of matter. Both forms of matter are eternal.[1]

Prior to creating our world, God the Father begat Spirit-Children (in association with the divine Mother).[2] In a sense, each of his Spirit-Children is eternal, in that they were formed from Spirit, which is eternal.[3] In another sense, they are not eternal; the Father begat them at a point in time – perhaps *formed* them would be a better way of describing what happened.[4] Jehovah was the first-born of the Father's Spirit-Children. Lucifer was the second. In some accounts, Adam and Eve were the third and fourth. All human beings existed as Spirit-Children of the Father prior to their physical birth. Human beings have no memories from that period because memories are suppressed at birth.[5]

Sometime after the Father formed his Spirit-Children, he convened a "Council in heaven" in order to propose a plan by which his Spirit-Children could be exalted and hence become gods.[6] Jehovah, his first-born, volunteered to carry out the Father's plan, and so earned the Father's favor. Lucifer opposed the Father's plan and proposed an alternative plan which involved depriving all of the Father's Spirit-Children of their *moral agency*, that is, their freedom. When the Father rejected his plan, Lucifer rebelled and fell into evil.

After the Council approved the Father's plan, Jehovah was exalted to godhood. Then, in cooperation with the Father, he created the world and placed Adam and Eve in the Garden of Eden.

The Genesis account describes humanity as "in the image and likeness of God". Mormons do not take these words metaphorically. They take them literally. According to the Mormon faith we resemble God the Father, both literally and physically.

During the Old Testament period, Jehovah revealed himself to the Hebrew people by that name. Later, Jehovah was born as Jesus of Nazareth.

The contrasts between the two accounts could not be more clear. They are utterly and totally different, and yes, incompatible.

6.2. The Fall of Man

Again, we'll begin with the Christian account of the fall. In this case, orthodox Christian theology was worked out in conflict between two strong individuals: Pelagius and Augustine.[7]

Late in the 4th century, a British Christian named Pelagius moved to Rome, the center of Western Christianity. But he was NOT impressed! Rather, he was appalled by the dissipation and immorality he saw around him. Some time later, Pelagius read Augustine's book, *The Confessions*; again, he was appalled. In *The Confessions*, Augustine claimed that we humans are helpless in our fight against sin. Our natural capacities are simply not adequate; God's grace is essential. In response, Pelagius wrote a literary reply to defend the idea that we are, in fact, capable of living up to God's expectations. He suggested that we sin because we capitulate voluntarily to the influences around us! But, we could have done otherwise. Sin is neither inevitable nor unavoidable. Augustine replied by noting Paul's stark statements in 1 Corinthians 15: "...as in Adam, all died." *Total Depravity*, the name often given to Augustine's position, doesn't mean that human beings cannot do good nor that they are as bad as they could possibly be. It means simply that depravity, the propensity toward sin, pollutes our entire being. Nothing escapes its destructive impact. *Total* then means *pervasive*.

During the following two decades, the two theologians engaged in an intense literary conflict. But by the early 5th Century the Church had concluded that Augustine was correct: When Adam sinned, he damaged both himself and his posterity. At our birth, even though we had not yet sinned actively, we were already thoroughly and completely corrupted by the pollution of sin. Our decision to participate actively in sin was, therefore, only a matter of time.

The Church did not concur with Augustine's view that God predestined some to salvation. But the church DID agree that Adam's sin destroyed our capacity to live a righteous life; Adam's sin made us totally dependent upon God's grace.

About a hundred years later, a group of theologians suggested that while we could not avoid sin, we could (and should) actively seek for God. Many times, perhaps most times, God takes the initiative. But sometimes individuals do seek God actively. The Church rejected that idea and insisted that God *always* takes the initiative. Therefore, we cannot even seek God except in response to God's gracious calling.

Since the 6th century, then, the church has consistently taught two ideas:
- We are all thoroughly polluted by sin, and
- We cannot even seek God except in response to his gracious calling.

Logically, Joseph Smith had to oppose this perspective. If – as we saw above – the Father begat all human beings as Spirit-Children prior to the creation of the universe, the sin of Adam, the sin of one particular human being, could not pollute them all. Smith acknowledged that Adam's sins did expose him personally to corruption and death and that Adam, as the physical, human father of the entire human race, passed on that susceptibility to corruption and death to all of his posterity. Smith agreed that all of Adam's posterity would inherit that propensity from their ancestor. But, Smith insisted, human beings were not deprived of their freedom by Adam's sin nor of their capacity to live righteously. Their capacity for moral choice remained unimpaired. And hence, Smith agreed with Pelagius against Augustine.

Moreover, Smith held that the fall itself was actually *fortunate*. After being placed in the Garden of Eden, but prior to the fall, Adam and Eve were not able to bear children. More importantly, they were not able to progress toward personal exaltation to godhood. The Fall, Smith insisted, opened up the possibility of procreation – which was part of the Father's Plan – and of exaltation to godhood. And in that sense, the Fall was fortunate.

Moral agency, the capacity to respond to God's commands, is fundamental to Smith's theology. At the council of the Gods (mentioned previously), God the Father presented a plan, which included the Fall and the exaltation of some – but not all! – of his Spirit-Children. Lucifer disagreed; he promised to enable ALL of the Father's Spirit-Children to achieve exaltation. But the flaw in Lucifer's plan was simple: He proposed to over-ride human agency, human capacity to choose the good, and ultimately to choose God. In contrast, The Father's plan included moral agency; he held that human beings need to choose the good. The Fall, then, opened the possibility for human beings to affirm the Father's plan, and by so doing to gain exaltation.

Again, we must note the contrasts:

1. Orthodox Christianity insists that Adam's fall damaged (or destroyed – both positions are taught within the orthodox community) both his moral capacity and also that of his posterity. We all eventually sin because we were born with a damaged (or destroyed) moral capacity. Mormon Theology denies that our moral capacity is even damaged, and asserts that all human beings can choose to obey the moral law.

2. Orthodox Christianity denies that human beings existed with the Father prior to their birth. Mormon theology is built on and follows from their belief that all human beings were begotten as the Father's Spirit-Children, that we concurred with the Father's plan, and that we agreed to be born and take on a body.

---

[1] *Doctrine and Covenants* 93:29-36.

[2] "All men and women are in the similitude of the universal Father and Mother, and are literally the sons and daughters of Deity." President Joseph F. Smith, John R. Winder, Anthon H. Lund (First Presidency), quoted in Burton, *We Believe*, p. 690. Note that the document

Burton quotes is an "official statement of First Presidency," and hence the idea of a divine Mother seems to be a doctrine of the church. See also Bruce McConkie, *Mormon Doctrine*, "Mother in Heaven", p. 516.

[3] *Doctrine and Covenants*, 93:29.

[4] "King Follett Discourse," ibid, pp.352-54.

[5] *Gospel Principles*, p. 9.

[6] *Doctrine and Covenants* 29:36-38; 76:25-29; *Pearl of Great Price* Moses 4:1-4; *Gospel Principles,* 11.

[7] See Chapter 17 in Olsen, *The Story of Christian Theology* and Chapter 13 in Kelly, *Early Christian Doctrines*.

The Mormon Faith

7. The Person of Jesus Christ

As I noted previously, Jesus presented his followers with a puzzle: Who was he? Obviously, he was a human being. And yet, he also seemed divine. And because of those qualities, it proved hard to speak or write about him.

Again, we'll begin by reviewing the historical process that led to the orthodox Christian consensus. In this case, the discussions lasted from about 100 A.D. to the Council of Chalcedon in 451 A.D. (the Fourth Ecumenical Council) a period of about 350 years.[1] During the first 225 years (from 100 A.D. to the Council of Nicea in 325, the First Ecumenical Council) the Church focused on the nature of God. Then from 325 to 451, the Church grappled with the issue of how God (as defined by the Council of Nicea) could become human. In short, there was a two-step historical process. I covered the first step of that historical process that led to the Christian understanding of the trinity in section 5.2. According to orthodox Christianity, the doctrine of the trinity is an absolutely essential foundation for understanding the doctrine of the Incarnation.

During the 50 years after the council of Nicea, church politics and Christian theology ebbed and flowed; there were winners and losers. However, the details of that process aren't important here. What is important is the outcome. In 381, the church convened the Second Ecumenical Council, the Council of Constantinople. At that gathering, the Church re-affirmed its previous conclusions, but reflected additionally on the divine nature of the Holy Spirit. Since then, the church has never wavered in its commitment to the doctrine of the trinity. In fact, the Nicene Creed (a slight modification of the Creed of Nicea) that is often recited as part of worship services, was written at that second Ecumenical Council.

The discussions about how to explain the Incarnation occupied the Church's leaders at three Councils: the Council of Constantinople in 381 (already mentioned), The Council of Ephesus in 431 (the Third Ecumenical Council), and then, Council of Chalcedon in 451 (the Fourth Ecumenical Council). At Chalcedon, the Church concluded that Jesus Christ existed as a single person with two natures – divine and human.

In sum, the Church concluded that the Eternal Logos, the Son, the second person of the trinity, took on our humanity and was born by the Virgin Mary as Jesus of Nazareth.

Mormon theology also affirms the deity of Jesus Christ. In fact, the title page of The Book of Mormon asserts that "Jesus is the Christ, the Eternal God ..." However, the explanation provided by Mormon theology has little in common with traditional Christianity.

Stated briefly, Mormon theology asserts that Jesus of Nazareth was the Incarnation of Jehovah, God the Father's first Spirit-Child. Obviously this statement requires some clarification and elaboration.[2]

According to Mormon theology, the Father's first-born Spirit child was born as Jesus of Nazareth by the Virgin Mary. However, Mormons teach that Jesus was not only the Father's first-born Spirit-Child, but that he was also, literally, the physical child of the Father. Now I admit that the previous sentence is sexually "suggestive." It could be construed as a modern version of various Greek stories where the gods have sexual intercourse with human women. But let me be clear: Nothing in Mormon theology suggests that interpretation of the Incarnation. Mormons do teach that Jesus was literally, physically, the Son of his Father by the Virgin Mary. However, they insist that the process was mysterious – and leave it at that.[3]

For example, Bruce McConkie, a member of the Quorum of the Twelve Apostles, wrote:

> "All men (Christ included) were born as the sons of God in the spirit; one man (Christ only) was born as the Son of God in this mortal world. He is the Only Begotten in the flesh. God was his Father; Mary was his mother. His Father was an immortal man; his Mother was a mortal woman. He is the Son of God in the same literal, full, and complete sense in which he is the son of Mary. There is nothing symbolic or figurative about it. He is God's Almighty Son and as such is distinguished from the Father in the same way any son is a separate person from his father."[4]

Note that his strong statement doesn't intrude on the mystery. Stephen Robinson likewise affirms the same theology, but likewise leaves the mystery unexplained.

> "If Jesus was truly a human being, then he had forty-six chromosomes, a double strand of twenty-three. If he was truly human, he got one strand of twenty-three chromosomes from his mother. Where did the other strand come from, if not from the Father? I am not talking about a sexual conception ..., only a divine conception and a divine sonship."[5]

The contrasts between the traditional Christian account of the Incarnation and the Mormon account are striking. I'll highlight three major areas of disagreement.

First, orthodox Christian theology and Mormon theology differ over the definition and use of the word *eternal*.

Orthodox Christian theology holds that God is *eternal* and inherently *timeless*. That is, he is not temporal; he exists outside time. So, God existed, before time began *and* He will never cease to exist. God is considered to be eternal, because he had no beginning and will have no end. Most theologians hold that time actually began when God created the world.

Mormon theology denies that anything (including God the Father himself) is eternal in the sense that orthodox Christian defines that term. Remember that the material universe – which is inherently temporary – has always existed – in time. Time – like the universe itself – had no beginning.

In short, the two theological systems hold differing perspectives on the nature of time. As a consequence, they use the word "eternal" differently.

Second, orthodox Christian theology and Mormon theology differ over the origin of the Son. Orthodox Christian theology asserts that the Logos is eternal, that is, that the Logos had no beginning nor will he have an end. Mormon theology teaches that Jesus is *the Eternal God*. Note, however, that the phrase "Eternal God" cannot logically mean for Mormons what it means for traditional Christians. Mormon cosmology acknowledges that Jehovah, Jesus' name during his pre-existence, had a beginning in time, just like all of the Father's Spirit-

The Mormon Faith

Children. However, having been exalted to Godhood, Jehovah is now *eternal* in the Mormon sense of that term. He will never cease to be a God. In short, Mormon theology acknowledges that Jesus had a beginning at a point in time, that he was exalted to godhood at a point in time, but asserts that he will continue to be god forever.

This is a complex idea. Allow me to state the idea in a slightly different manner.

Historic Christian theology asserts that the Logos is eternally *begotten* by the Father. The *begetting* is not an event in time; rather, *begetting* refers to the nature of the Son's relationship with the Father. He is subordinate to the Father. The Son's subordination to the Father is an inherent part of God's complexity. And hence, the Father *eternally begets* the Son.

Mormon theology, in contrast, asserts that the Father begat all of his Spirit-Children at a point in time. And so, the Father existed temporally prior to his Spirit-Children generally, and more specifically, prior to Jehovah, his first-born Spirit-Child. Mormon theology can be construed, therefore, as a form of Arian theology, the theology condemned at the Council of Nicea. The Bishops at that Council crafted the complex phrases of the Creed of Nicea precisely to assert that the Father begat the Son and that the Son was begotten by the Father *before* time began.

Finally, in addition to these theological differences, Mormon theology includes a series of ideas which have no counterpart in historic Christianity: the Council of the Gods prior to creation, pre-existent souls, the idea that Jesus is the *Elder Brother* of all human beings, and the idea that Lucifer is Jesus' younger brother.

Traditional orthodox Christianity and the Mormon Faith both proclaim a *story* in order to explain the origins of Jesus of Nazareth. But the two stories are radically different.

---

[1] The material in the next few paragraphs section is condensed from Part IV of Olsen, *The Story of Christian Theology* and Chapters 11 & 12 of Kelly, *Early Christian Doctrine*.
[2] *Gospel Principles*, Ch. 3.
[3] *Book of Mormon*, Alma 7:10.
[4] Quoted in Blomberg & Robinson, *How Wide the Divide?* p. 122. See also p. 135.
[5] Ibid, p. 139.

8. The Nature of our Salvation

When human beings meet God and are forgiven, what exactly happens? In reply to that question, the Church has used a variety of terms: We are redeemed, regenerated, and justified – to mention a few of those terms. However, the Western church has tended to focus on the term *justification*.

That term is key to understanding Paul's *Letter to the Romans*. Moreover, five hundred years ago, Luther was willing – literally – to go to the stake over his interpretation of Paul's theology of justification. In response to the Lutheran critique of the Catholic doctrine of justification, the Roman Catholic Church was forced to call the Council of Trent, which was convened just a couple years before Luther's death. Since that Council, the western church – that is Roman Catholics and Protestants – have debated the nature of justification almost continually – sometimes caustically.

During that same period, few western theologians bothered to comment on the term *deification*.[1] And that fact is fascinating! Eastern Orthodox churches have always focused on deification, rather than justification. Moreover, the discussion of deification began in the 2nd century so it's not exactly a novelty! But because the term is so unfamiliar to us in the west, it sounds vaguely pernicious.

Christians are committed to the idea that the divine nature and the human nature can be joined in one person. After all, since the Council of Chalcedon in 451, Christians have claimed that those two natures were joined in the person of Jesus Christ. But western theologians don't generally spend much time reflecting on the implications of that fact for our salvation. However, the New Testament clearly teaches that Christians become partakers of the divine nature (1 Peter). Moreover, Christians receive the gift of the Holy Spirit. So what does that mean for us?

I don't intend to discuss *deification* extensively. After all, this isn't a theology textbook. I intend to do here exactly what I've done in previous chapters: explain in very general terms what the church teaches and then explain how the Mormon Faith adapts and modifies those ideas.

The western church has always taught that we humans were created in the image and likeness of God. (Genesis 1) In the Fall, depending on your theology, that image was either damaged or destroyed. The Eastern Churches understand salvation as the restoration of the image of God. They use the term *deification* to describe that process.

In Chapter 5, I pointed out that Christian theology has always insisted on the distinction between the Creator and the creation. And that includes Eastern theology. The Eastern Orthodox theologians NEVER thought of deification as bridging that gulf.[2]

Joseph Smith taught a theology of *exaltation*, that humans have the capacity of becoming gods. Moreover, God the Father himself is an *exalted human being*.[3]

Those two ideas are profoundly contrary to the Christian Faith. First, the Bible does not teach them. Second, it undermines the distinction between the Creator and the creation. And third, neither of Joseph Smith's ideas makes sense. If God the Father and human beings are of the same species, then there never was a gulf between them, and *exaltation* amounts to a promotion.

The Mormon Faith

In *How Wide the Divide?* Robinson states that " ... Latter-day Saints maintain that God's work is to *remove* the distinctions and barriers between us and to make us what God is."[4] He, of course, is free to make such a claim. But he needs to remember that the Church NEVER intended *deification* to imply that the process of salvation abolished the distinction between the Creator and the creation.

In *Are Mormons Christians?* Robinson argues:

> "Critics of the Latter-day Saints may respond that the early Christian saints, the later Greek theologians, and C. S. Lewis all understand the doctrine of deification differently than the Latter-day Saints do, but this is untrue in the case of the early Christians and C. S. Lewis. Anyway, such a response amounts to a quibble ..."[5]

Allow me to suggest that removing the distinction between the Creator and the creation is not a *quibble*. That distinction is at the *core of the faith*.[6]

---

[1] For example, Erickson's work, *Christian Theology*, doesn't discuss the idea. Moreover, it doesn't even include the term deification in the index.

[2] If you are interested in pursuing the idea, I'd recommend: *Theosis: Deification in Christian Theology*, ed. by Stephen Finlan and Vladimir Kharlamov (Pickwick Publications, 2006).

[3] See section 5.3. and the footnotes for that section.

[4] *How Wide the Divide?* by Craig L. Blomberg and Stephen E. Robinson, p. 81.

[5] *Are Mormons Christians?* by Stephen E. Robinson, p. 64.

[6] See footnote 3 of Chapter 5 where Richard Mouw asserts that the distinction between the Creator and the creatures is at the core of the Christian Faith.

9. Theological Reflections

9.1. Theological Conclusions

As I promised, the previous four chapters laid out a series of contrasts to show where and how orthodox Christianity and the Mormon Faith differ. It would be hard to exaggerate the differences. <u>The two theologies seem to have little in common other than a remarkably similar vocabulary.</u>

True, there are other topics which could be discussed. In addition to the four major doctrines discussed above, orthodox Christians and Mormons differ about a variety of interesting theological issues. For example, Mormons hold unique views about baptism, including their doctrine of *Baptism for the Dead*. They teach that there are three levels in Heaven. They believe in *Eternal Marriage* or *Sealing*, as noted above. And when Mormons and Christians dialog, they often discuss their respective views of faith and grace. Moreover, orthodox Christians and Mormons disagree about a whole variety of historical issues: such as, whether the historical account contained in *The Book of Mormon* is reliable and whether it's possible to reconcile Smith's various accounts of his visions.

But as I indicated in the Introduction, I intend to bypass those questions and focus on theology. So, in conclusion, I want to raised two questions explicitly and offer my personal replies.

9.2. Is the Mormon Church a restoration of early Christianity?

Joseph Smith taught that true Christianity was lost toward the end of the first century when the early Christian church fell into apostasy – the Mormon doctrine of *The Great Apostasy*. If he was correct, the development and growth of Christian theology from the second century onward was built on an apostate theological foundation. Consequently the conclusions of the Council of Nicea and the Council of Chalcedon need to be discarded and ignored.

As a Christian, I'd like to make three observations:

First, Smith's argument that early Christianity fell into apostasy is an argument from silence. There is quite literally no historical evidence whatsoever – literally not one shred of evidence – to support his position. Rather, the available documents show a gradual development in Christian thinking.

Second, there is simply no room, historically, for *The Great Apostasy*. According to tradition, the Apostle John, the Biblical author, died in Ephesus about 95 A.D. The Apostolic Father, Clement of Rome, flourished about that same time. Ignatius of Antioch was martyred in Rome about 105 A.D. In short, the literary evidence we have shows a smooth transition from the Biblical writers to the early Christian theological writers.

Third, Smith's statement that his theology restored the lost theology of early Christianity is also an argument from silence. There is absolutely no evidence whatsoever to support the idea that the Mormon theological positions described in the previous chapters restored pristine Christianity.

Smith, of course, asserted that his restored theology was based on revelations provided by the Angel Moroni. But again, we are faced with a simple assertion. The golden plates that Smith claimed to have recovered are no longer available.

In short, Mormon theology rests solely and simply on Joseph Smith's assertions. Personally, I would suggest that the total lack of evidence for *The Great Apostasy* should lead one to reject the Mormon understanding of early Christian history.

9.3. Is Mormon theology Christian?

Orthodox Christians, when presented with Mormon theology, are incredulous. Their reaction is, "How could you mistake this for authentic Christianity?"

Mormons theologians, in contrast, ask a different series of questions: "How can you deny that we are Christian when we believe in God the Father, God the Son, and God the Holy Spirit; when we believe that salvation is by grace through faith; when we insist that baptism is important? Surely, Mormons fit within the historic Christian Faith!"

In order to sort this out, I'll need to ask you to focus on definitions again.

Both orthodox Christians and Mormons agree with the following theological statement: **Jesus is the Eternal Son of God**. But when you expand the statement to include the theological foundations of each system, you end up with two, totally incompatible statements.

Orthodox Christian theology holds that:

> **Jesus** (the human being, conceived by the Holy Spirit and born of the Virgin Mary)
> **is the Eternal** (that is, he existed from eternity past and he will continue to exist for all eternity; he always was)
> **Son of God** (that is, He is the *Logos*, the second person of the trinity, begotten eternally by God the Father).

Mormon theology holds that:

> **Jesus** (the pre-existent Spirit-Child of the Father, called Jehovah in the Old Testament, who agreed – like all Spirit-Children of the Father – to be born as a human being in order to be embodied – and in his case, to be born as the physical child of God the Father and the Virgin Mary)
> **is the Eternal** (that is, he was in fact brought into existence by the Father at a point in time as a Spirit-Child; however, having been exalted to godhood prior to his incarnation, he will live forever; and hence he is now eternal)
> **Son of God** (he is both the first-born Spirit-Child and also the physical child of God the Father)

The words are the same. But the theological exposition of those words is utterly and entirely different. In my opinion, attempting to say that both theological positions are "Christian" simply doesn't make sense. As the various contrasts I've provided show clearly, the two theological perspectives are starkly different; they assert fundamentally different world-views.

It is, in my opinion, futile to try to find a common word for two such different theologies. It's simply not reasonable to hold that historic orthodox Christianity and Mormon theology are both Christian. Consequently, I would conclude that the Mormon Faith is not an expression of Christianity.

9.4. If Mormon theology is not Christian, then what is it – from an orthodox Christian perspective?

The Mormon Church has been called a *cult* and a *sect*. Neither word has a clear definition. Moreover, both are strong, pejorative words. Using them has not helped the two sides of the divide understand each other very well. I'd suggest we refuse to use those terms.

We need a term that has a reasonably clear definition, and preferably a term that has been used widely in the history of the Church. I'd suggest the term *heresy* meets that standard.

I know, of course, that my Mormon readers are not going to like that term much better than the two terms I've rejected. Nonetheless, we need a term of some sort in order to carry on an orderly discussion.

In early Christian history, there were two great heresies: Gnosticism and Manichaeism. Gnosticism originated in the late 1st century or the early 2nd century and was opposed by the Church almost immediately with great vigor.[1] The perspective has reared its head occasionally since then (most notably – and recently – in *The Da Vinci Code* [2]). But for practical purposes, Gnosticism was vanquished by the 4th century. Manichaeism is a dualistic perspective (somewhat like modern Zoroastrianism) that originated in Persia in the 3rd century. Augustine attacked it vigorously. It too survived for several centuries. Indeed, some historians hold that the 11th century Cathari were really remnants of Manichaeism. But it too was vanquished.

So why are those two theologies considered to be heresies? Gnosticism and Manichaeism both:
- claimed to be Christian
- used Christian vocabulary extensively, but
- redefined orthodox Christian terms in ways that made their theologies utterly incompatible with orthodox Christianity.

The Mormon Faith fits that pattern – exactly. The Mormon Church claims to be Christian, and Mormon theology uses a large number of Christian terms. But as the contrasts I've provided show, Mormon theology redefines those Christian terms in ways that are utterly and totally inconsistent with orthodox Christian theology. Therefore, it seems to me appropriate to conclude that the Mormon Faith is a contemporary Christian heresy.

9.5. How should orthodox Christians respond to the Mormon claim?

First of all, Orthodox Christians will need to continue their opposition to this contemporary heresy, just as early Christians opposed early heresies. Orthodox Christians should listen politely and respectfully to Mormon claims. But when all is said and done, Christians should simply deny that those claims are justified.

Second, allow me to reiterate a comment from Chapter 1, the Introduction. You cannot minister to a person you don't love. Theological arguments rarely "win the day". The theology I've presented here provides the context for fruitful discussions. But theology, even if correct, is no substitute for reaching out in love. And that remains the primary task.

---

[1] See "The Gnostic Way," *Early Christian Doctrines* by J. N. D. Kelly, pp. 22-29; chapters 1 & 4 in *The Story of Christian Theology* by Roger Olsen deal with Gnosticism.

[2] Dan Brown. *The Da Vinci Code*. Doubleday, 2003

Suggested Reading

Basic Reading on Orthodox Christianity

Biblical Studies:

Anderson, Bernhard W., Steven Bishop, Judith Newman. *Understanding the Old Testament* (Prentice Hall, 2006).

Bartholomew, Graig G. and Michael W. Goheen. *The Drama of Scripture: Finding Our Place in the Biblical Story.* Baker, 2004. A short "Prologue" provides a clearly written introduction to reading the Bible as the narrative of God's Redemptive work. Then the rest of the book takes the Reader from Genesis 1 and the story of creation to the end of the New Testament … and then with a jump to the end of time! … to the completion of Redemption.

Church History:

Latourette, Kenneth Scott. *A History of Christianity.* Harper & Row, 1953. This book is a classic "door stop" of a book that contains about 1500 pages. But if you want a reference book, this would be an excellent choice.

Shelly, Bruce. *Church History in Plain Language.* Word, 1982. There are many such histories, but Shelley's book is a fine place to begin.

Walker, Williston. *A History of the Christian Church.* Scribner. This is a standard textbook on Church history. It was originally written in 1918, but has been updated several times. The most recent edition is from 1985.

History of Theology:

Kelly, J. N. D. *Early Christian Doctrines*. Continuum, 5th edition, 1977. Kelly's work has been a standard for over a generation. It's hard to beat his account of the first five centuries of Christian theology.

Lohse, Bernhard. *A Short History of Christian Doctrine: From the First Century to the Present*. Fortress, 1966. Lohse's book has been in print for a generation! The chapters that cover the period from the First Century to the Reformation are superb. The last few chapters, which cover the Post-Reformation period, don't have the same clarity.

Olsen, Roger. *The Story of Christian Theology: Twenty Centuries of Tradition and Reform*. IVP Academic, 1999. Very readable history of doctrine; he manages to make some fairly complex history understandable.

Quash, Ben and Michael Ward. *Heresies and How to Avoid Them: Why it matters what Christians Believe*. SPCK, 2007. A short and accessible introduction to the major heresies the church faced during the period 100 A. D. to 600 A.D.

Systematic Theology:

Erickson, Millard. *Christian Theology*. Baker, 1985. A good reference book from a conservative Evangelical position

General Works of Interest:

Each of the following four books is a "classic," including the most recent by N. T. Wright. Each explains what it means to be Christian for the layperson.

Chesterton. Gilbert K. *Orthodoxy*. Various editions. First published in 1908.

Lewis, C. S. *Mere Christianity*. Various editions. First published in 1952.

Stott, John R. W. *Basic Christianity*. Various Editions. First published in 1958

Wright, N. T. *Simply Christian; Why Christianity makes Sense*. Harper, 2006.

Basic Reading on the Mormon Faith

Mormon History and theology

Primary Sources:
The Book of Mormon; Another Testament of Jesus Christ. The Doctrine and Covenants of the Church of Jesus Christ of Latter-day Saints. The Pearl of Great Price. These three works are held by Latter-day Saints to be inspired. They are available in a wide variety of formats.

Teachings of the Prophet Joseph Smith. Compiled by Joseph Fielding Smith. Deseret, 1976.

Reference Works:
The material in both of the following works is arranged alphabetically (rather than logically or topically).

Burton, Rulon R. *We Believe: Doctrines and Principles of The Church of Jesus Christ of Latter-day Saints*. Tabernacle Books, 2004. Burton's book is an extensive collection of quotations. The author indicates in the introduction that he has included only quotations from authoritative sources – and hence that his book can be taken as an authoritative statement of Mormon theology.

McConkie, Bruce R. *Mormon Doctrine*. Deseret Book, 1979. McConkie was asked to join the Quorum of the Twelve in 1972 – the highest ranking body in the Mormon Church – which makes him something of an authority. His book provides his personal perspective on the Mormon faith.

Mormon History:

Bushman, Claudia Lauper and Richard Lyman Bushman. *Building the Kingdom: A History of Mormons in America*. Oxford, 2001.

Mormon Theological Works:

Gospel Principles. This statement of Mormon theology is an official publication of the LDS church and intended for the education and training of LDS members. It's widely available and commonly used.

Millet, Robert L. *A Different Jesus; the Christ of the Latter-Day Saints*. Eerdmans, 2005.

Millet, Robert L. *The Mormon Faith; A New Look at Christianity*. Shadow Mountain, 1998.

Robinson, Stephen E. *Are Mormons Christians?* Bookcraft, 1991.

Talmage, James E. *A Study of the Articles of Faith*. Deseret, 1890.

Mormon-Evangelical Dialogs

For the record, Blomberg, McDermott and Johnson are the Evangelicals, while Robinson and Millet are the Mormons. The discussions are handled politely – but also pointedly in some cases.

Blomberg, Craig L. and Stephen E. Robinson. *How Wide the Divide: A Mormon & an Evangelical in Conversation.* InterVarsity Press, 1997.
Millet, Robert L. and Gerald R. McDermott. *Claiming Christ: A Mormon-Evangelical Debate.* Brazos Press, 2007.
Millet, Robert L. and Gregory C. V. Johnson. *Bridging the Divide: The Continuing Conversation between a Mormon and an Evangelical.* Monkfish Books. 2007.

About the Author

After completing an undergraduate degree in Anthropology at Wheaton College (IL) and graduating from seminary (Trinity Evangelical Divinity School in IL), Dr. William Wells began his studies for a Ph.D. in Philosophy and Religion at Syracuse University. Upon completing his doctorate in 1970, he taught at the University of Hawaii, Hilo College and later at both Regent College (Vancouver, B.C.), and the Graduate School of Theology at Wheaton College. In his forties, Dr. Wells left academia and a few years later joined Wycliffe Bible Translators. Now retired after twenty years of service with Wycliffe, he lives in Southern California, where he teaches and writes.

Other books by the author:

A Brief Introduction to the Bible

Faith of Our Fathers: An Introduction to the Evangelicals

The author is open to dialog and discussion. You may contact him at:

William40Wells@gmail.com

Made in the USA
Charleston, SC
16 March 2010